TEACHING

Life IS Good

An Interactive Book Designed to Build Children's
Self-Esteem, Confidence, Character and Lifelong Success

Attach Your Picture Here

By

Eric Alexander Crawford

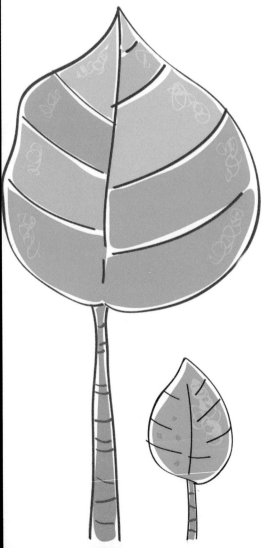

ISBN: 0692283684
ISBN-13: 9780692283684
By Eric Alexander Crawford
Edited by Karyn Lindberg
Published by RDC New York

A note to adults:

Teaching Kids Life IS Good is the best-selling book that helps children build a fun and inspiring foundation of character, confidence, and self-esteem. The secret to its effectiveness is the pairing of positive statements with pictures of your child that you attach on each page. These images provide a captivating and powerful way for children to personalize and absorb the uplifting messages throughout the book. When read on a consistent basis, the ideas take root and prepare children for a lifetime of success and fulfillment.

Many adults spend a lifetime overcoming limiting beliefs and personality traits that were unconsciously picked up in those impressionable younger years. Much of that can be saved by deliberately building winning outlooks early in life. This book is designed to do just that.

Teaching Kids Life IS Good is ideal for ages 2 - 12 while children are still within their most formative years of subconscious development. Some children will prefer to design and read the book on their own. Others will enjoy choosing the pictures and spending quality time reading it aloud each night with family and friends.

Teaching Kids Life IS Good makes a great gift that children will cherish always.

Here's how it works: Wherever you see placeholder frames like the one below which says *attach your picture here*, tape or paste your child's photo over the frame to personalize each page just for them. The goal is to match the vibe of each picture as best as possible to the statements on each page, but not to worry about getting it perfect. The pictures can be updated as often as desired, and it is ok if your photos are larger or smaller than our frames. If you don't already have pictures, you can take some just for this book. If you're not sure what pictures to choose, any happy pictures will be great :-)

Dedication

To every child who will grow up with

a healthy sense of

confidence, character, and self-esteem.

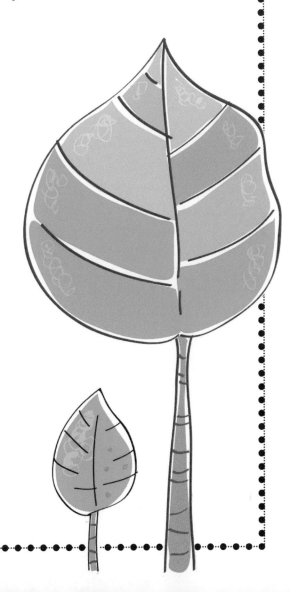

I am alive for a
positive purpose.

attach
Your Picture
Here

I am loving
and I am loved.

I like helping people.

Attach Your Picture Here

People enjoy helping me.

I am a good friend to others.

I treat others how I
would like to be treated.

I am strong and confident.

I can handle all
of life's challenges.

I see the good in
other people.

I enjoy when
others succeed.

I am thankful for the
friends in my life.

Attach
Your Picture
Here

I appreciate the
things in my life.

I love to learn.

Attach
Your Picture
Here

I am smart
and creative.

I am patient and
forgiving to others.

Others are patient
and forgiving to me.

I am joyful.

I like to look on the
bright side of life.

I like meeting new people.

I smile and look at others
when talking with them.

I am reliable and do my best.

Attach
Your Picture
Here

I am trustworthy.

Things are always working together for my good.

attach Your Picture Here

I can succeed at whatever I set my attention to.

Reflection:

What good did I experience today?

Reflection:

What good can come tomorrow?

My life is full of:

Joy   Forgiveness

Inspiration   Patience

Love   Appreciation

Integrity   Gratitude

Self-Control   Gentleness

Peace   Focus

Compassion   Goodness

Kindness   Understanding

Generosity   Faithfulness

Humility   & Positivity

I focus on whatever is **noble, right, pure, good, admirable, excellent, and worthy of praise!**

My Life IS Good!

Eric is a business leader and youth mentor. His wife Cher is an elementary school teacher. Both hold master's degrees and have years of experience empowering children to live their best lives. During that time they learned much of how a child adapts to life has to do with the impression they develop about themselves and the world at a young age. Because of that, they created this fun and innovative book to help children develop a healthy, positive, and well-adjusted sense of confidence, character, and self-esteem. All for the joys and satisfaction of lifelong success.

Made in the USA
Monee, IL
25 January 2020